LEADERSHIP OF CONVENIENCE

Chapter 1 : Introduction

Leadership is a crucial aspect of any organization or community. Effective leadership can inspire, motivate, and guide a group towards success. Leaders are responsible for setting goals, making decisions, and managing resources to achieve those goals. However, not all leadership is genuine, and not all leaders prioritize the well-being of their followers.

This book will explore the concept of leadership of convenience and its negative consequences. Leadership of convenience refers to leaders who prioritize their own convenience over the well-being of their followers. These leaders are primarily concerned with their personal gain rather than the success of their organization or community. They may bend rules, make short-sighted decisions, and disregard the needs of others. Leaders who engage in leadership of convenience may also display narcissistic tendencies and create a culture of fear and mistrust.

In this book, we will examine the negative consequences of leadership of convenience and the importance of true leadership. True leadership involves prioritizing the well-being of one's followers over one's own convenience. Effective leaders focus on the long-term success of their organization or community and make decisions that benefit everyone, not just themselves. True leaders also foster a culture of trust, collaboration, and mutual respect.

We will also discuss the characteristics of true leaders and how they can be developed. True leaders possess certain characteristics that set them apart from leaders of convenience. These characteristics include vision, empathy, integrity, humility, and courage. True leadership is a skill that can be developed through education and practice.

The purpose of this book is to help leaders recognize the negative consequences of leadership of convenience and inspire them to become true leaders. We believe that true leadership is essential for the success of any organization or community. By fostering a culture of trust, collaboration, and mutual respect, true leaders can inspire their followers to be more productive, engaged, and motivated. We hope that this book will serve as a guide for aspiring leaders and inspire them to become true leaders who prioritize the well-being of their followers over their own convenience.

Chapter 2 : What is Leadership of Convenience?

Leadership of convenience is a style of leadership that prioritizes the convenience of the leader over the well-being of their followers. Leaders who engage in leadership of convenience are primarily concerned with their own personal gain rather than the success of their organization or community. This type of leadership is often characterized by short-sighted decision-making, bending rules, and disregarding the needs of others.

Leadership of convenience can manifest in various ways. For example, leaders who engage in this type of leadership may prioritize their own comfort over the needs of their followers. They may take excessive vacations, work shorter hours than their subordinates, or assign themselves the easiest tasks. They may also bend rules or take shortcuts to achieve their goals, even if it harms their followers or the organization as a whole.

Leaders who engage in leadership of convenience may also display narcissistic tendencies. They may believe that they are always right and refuse to consider other viewpoints. They may prioritize their own interests over the interests of others and display a lack of empathy for their followers. This type of leadership can create a culture of fear and mistrust, where followers feel undervalued and disrespected.

One of the most significant negative consequences of leadership of convenience is that it undermines the trust and respect that followers have for their leader. When leaders prioritize their own convenience over the well-being of their followers, it sends a message that they do not value or respect their followers. This can lead to a lack of motivation, engagement, and commitment among followers, which can ultimately harm the organization or community.

Another negative consequence of leadership of convenience is that it can lead to short-sighted decision-making. Leaders who prioritize their own convenience may be more likely to make decisions that benefit them in the short term but harm the organization or community in the long term. They may also be less likely to take the time to consider the perspectives and needs of others when making decisions, which can result in poor decision-making.

In contrast, true leadership involves prioritizing the well-being of one's followers over one's own convenience. Effective leaders focus on the long-term success of their organization or community and make decisions that benefit everyone, not just themselves. True leaders foster a culture of trust, collaboration, and mutual respect, which inspires their followers to be more productive, engaged, and motivated.

In conclusion, leadership of convenience is a style of leadership that prioritizes the convenience of the leader over the well-being of their followers. Leaders who engage in this type of leadership may prioritize their own comfort over the needs of their followers, display narcissistic tendencies, and create a culture of fear and mistrust. The negative consequences of leadership of convenience include a lack of trust and respect among followers, short-sighted decision-making, and a lack of motivation, engagement, and commitment among followers.

Chapter 3: Psychology of "Leaders of Convenience"

Leadership is a complex phenomenon influenced by various psychological factors. While many leaders are driven by a genuine commitment to their group or organization, there is a distinct category known as "Leaders of Convenience." These individuals assume leadership roles primarily for personal gain or convenience, lacking a sincere dedication to the collective goals and welfare of the group. Understanding the psychology behind leaders of convenience is crucial in uncovering their motivations, behaviors, and potential consequences. This article delves into the psychology of leaders of convenience, shedding light on the underlying factors that contribute to their emergence.

Self-Centeredness and Ego:

At the core of leaders of convenience lies self-centeredness. They prioritize their own needs, desires, and personal benefits over the well-being of the group. Their ego-centric approach often results in a lack of empathy and consideration for the concerns and perspectives of others. Instead of nurturing a collaborative and inclusive environment, these leaders tend to view their position as a means to fulfill their own aspirations, often neglecting the collective interests.

Opportunism and Selective Leadership:

Leaders of convenience exhibit a strong sense of opportunism. They carefully choose leadership roles that offer immediate advantages, such as social status, financial gains, or recognition.

Rather than taking on challenging or demanding positions that require personal sacrifice or effort, they opt for opportunities that provide the most benefits with the least amount of inconvenience. Their selective approach to leadership further reinforces their self-serving nature.

Risk Aversion and Comfort Zone:

Leaders of convenience tend to be risk-averse. They shy away from situations involving uncertainty, potential failure, or conflicts. Such leaders prefer maintaining the status quo rather than challenging it. This aversion to risk is rooted in their desire to preserve personal comfort and avoid potential negative consequences. Consequently, they may avoid taking on leadership roles that require them to make difficult decisions or confront challenging issues, hindering the growth and progress of the group they lead.

Lack of Commitment and Inconsistency:

A distinguishing feature of leaders of convenience is their lack of commitment and inconsistency in their leadership roles. Genuine leaders display dedication and consistency, striving to nurture the growth and development of their group or organization. In contrast, leaders of convenience exhibit a pattern of withdrawing from responsibilities when faced with difficulties or conflicts. They prioritize personal comfort and convenience, failing to provide the necessary support and guidance that genuine leadership demands.

Desire for Control and Power:

Some leaders of convenience are driven by a desire for control and power. They view leadership as a means to exert influence and manipulate others for personal gain. They may undermine the contributions and ideas of others, seeking to maintain their authority and control over the group. This power-oriented approach often erodes trust, collaboration, and the overall well-being of the group.

Psychological Rationalization:

Leaders of convenience may not always be aware of their own motivations or the negative impact of their behaviors. In many cases, they rationalize their actions as being in the best interest of the group or organization. This psychological mechanism allows them to justify their self-serving approach and avoid confronting their lack of genuine commitment. By distorting reality and minimizing the importance of collective goals, they perpetuate their convenience-driven leadership style.

Chapter 4 : The Negative Consequences of Leadership of Convenience

Leadership of convenience can have significant negative consequences for both leaders and their followers. In this chapter, we will explore some of the most significant negative consequences of leadership of convenience.

1. Loss of trust and respect

One of the most significant negative consequences of leadership of convenience is the loss of trust and respect among followers. When leaders prioritize their own convenience over the well-being of their followers, it sends a message that they do not value or respect their followers. This can lead to a lack of motivation, engagement, and commitment among followers, which can ultimately harm the organization or community. When followers lose trust and respect for their leader, it can be challenging to regain it, and the leader may struggle to lead effectively.

2. Poor decision-making

Leadership of convenience can also lead to poor decision-making. Leaders who prioritize their own convenience may be more likely to make decisions that benefit them in the short term but harm the organization or community in the long term. They may also be less likely to take the time to consider the perspectives and needs of others when making decisions, which can result in poor decision-making. Poor decision-making can ultimately harm the organization or community and lead to a lack of trust and respect among followers.

3. Lack of motivation, engagement, and commitment

Leadership of convenience can also lead to a lack of motivation, engagement, and commitment among followers. When leaders prioritize their own convenience over the well-being of their followers, it sends a message that the followers are not valued or respected. This can lead to a lack of motivation, engagement, and commitment among followers, which can ultimately harm the organization or community. When followers do not feel valued or respected, they may be less likely to go above and beyond in their work, which can harm the organization or community.

4. Culture of fear and mistrust

Leadership of convenience can also create a culture of fear and mistrust. When leaders prioritize their own convenience, it can create an environment where followers are afraid to speak up or share their opinions. They may feel undervalued and disrespected, which can create a culture of fear and mistrust. When followers are afraid to speak up, it can lead to a lack of innovation and creativity, which can ultimately harm the organization or community.

5. High turnover rates

Leadership of convenience can also lead to high turnover rates. When followers do not feel valued or respected, they may be more likely to leave the organization or community. This can lead to a high turnover rate, which can be costly for the organization or community. High turnover rates can also harm the organization or community's reputation, making it more challenging to attract and retain top talent.

Leadership of convenience can have significant negative consequences for both leaders and their followers. These negative consequences include a loss of trust and respect, poor decision-making, a lack of motivation, engagement, and commitment, a culture of fear and mistrust, and high turnover rates.

Chapter 5 : The Importance of True Leadership

True leadership is essential for the success of any organization or community. Unlike leadership of convenience, true leadership prioritizes the well-being of the followers over the convenience of the leader. In this chapter, we will explore the importance of true leadership and how it can benefit both leaders and their followers.

1. Building trust and respect

True leadership is built on a foundation of trust and respect. When leaders prioritize the well-being of their followers over their own convenience, it sends a message that they value and respect their followers. This can lead to a culture of trust and respect, where followers are more likely to be engaged, motivated, and committed. When followers trust and respect their leader, they are more likely to follow their vision and work together towards a common goal.

2. Encouraging innovation and creativity

True leadership also encourages innovation and creativity. When leaders prioritize the well-being of their followers, they create an environment where followers feel valued and empowered to share their ideas and perspectives. This can lead to new and innovative ideas that can benefit the organization or community. True leaders also encourage their followers to take risks and try new things, which can lead to new opportunities and growth.

3. Fostering collaboration and teamwork

True leadership also fosters collaboration and teamwork. When leaders prioritize the well-being of their followers, they create a culture of collaboration and mutual respect. This can lead to more effective teamwork and problem-solving, as followers feel comfortable sharing their ideas and perspectives. True leaders also encourage their followers to work together towards a common goal, which can lead to a sense of unity and shared purpose.

4. Making ethical and moral decisions

True leadership also involves making ethical and moral decisions. When leaders prioritize the well-being of their followers, they consider the ethical and moral implications of their decisions. They strive to make decisions that benefit the organization or community as a whole, rather than just themselves. True leaders also take responsibility for their decisions and actions, and they hold themselves accountable to their followers.

5. Building a positive culture and reputation

True leadership can also help to build a positive culture and reputation for the organization or community. When leaders prioritize the well-being of their followers, it creates a culture of trust, respect, collaboration, and innovation. This can lead to a positive reputation for the organization or community, which can attract top talent and resources. A positive culture can also help to retain top talent and promote growth and success.

In conclusion, true leadership is essential for the success of any organization or community. It prioritizes the well-being of the followers over the convenience of the leader and fosters a culture of trust, respect, collaboration, and innovation. True leaders encourage their followers to work together towards a common goal, make ethical and moral decisions, and build a positive culture and reputation. By prioritizing true leadership, organizations and communities can achieve long-term success and growth.

Chapter 6 : Characteristics of True Leaders

True leaders possess a distinct set of characteristics that differentiate them from leaders of convenience. In this chapter, we will explore some of the key characteristics of true leaders.

1. Visionary

True leaders are visionary, meaning they have a clear and compelling vision of the future. They are able to articulate this vision in a way that inspires and motivates their followers. This vision provides direction and purpose, helping to align the efforts of the organization or community towards a common goal.

2. Empathetic

True leaders are empathetic, meaning they are able to understand and share the feelings of their followers. They are able to put themselves in their followers' shoes, which helps them to make decisions that are in their followers' best interests. This empathy also fosters a culture of trust and respect, as followers feel valued and understood.

3. Decisive

True leaders are decisive, meaning they are able to make tough decisions quickly and effectively. They are able to weigh the pros and cons of different options and make a decision based on what is best for the organization or community as a whole. This decisiveness also helps to maintain momentum and progress towards the organization's goals.

4. Authentic

True leaders are authentic, meaning they are genuine and honest in their interactions with others. They are true to themselves and their values, and they are not afraid to admit their mistakes or vulnerabilities. This authenticity fosters a culture of openness and transparency, which helps to build trust and respect among followers.

5. Inspirational

True leaders are inspirational, meaning they are able to inspire and motivate their followers to achieve their full potential. They lead by example, modeling the behavior and values they expect from their followers. This inspiration can help to create a sense of shared purpose and a commitment to the organization's goals.

6. Accountable

True leaders are accountable, meaning they take responsibility for their decisions and actions. They hold themselves to high standards of integrity and ethical behavior, and they are willing to admit when they have made a mistake. This accountability helps to build trust and respect among followers, and it fosters a culture of responsibility and ownership.

7. Lifelong Learners

True leaders are lifelong learners, meaning they are constantly seeking to improve themselves and their leadership skills. They are open to feedback and constructive criticism, and they actively seek out new opportunities for growth and development. This commitment to continuous learning helps to foster a culture of innovation and growth within the organization or community.

In conclusion, true leaders possess a distinct set of characteristics that set them apart from leaders of convenience.

They are visionary, empathetic, decisive, authentic, inspirational, accountable, and committed to lifelong learning. By embodying these characteristics, true leaders are able to inspire and motivate their followers towards a common goal, fostering a culture of trust, respect, collaboration, and innovation.

Chapter 7 : Developing True Leadership

While some individuals may possess natural leadership abilities, true leadership is a skill that can be developed over time. In this chapter, we will explore some of the ways in which individuals can develop their leadership skills and become true leaders.

1. Seek Out Leadership Opportunities

One of the best ways to develop leadership skills is to seek out opportunities to lead. This can be in the form of taking on a leadership role within an organization, volunteering for leadership positions in your community, or simply taking on leadership responsibilities within your current job. By putting yourself in a position to lead, you will have the opportunity to practice and develop your leadership skills.

2. Learn from Others

Another way to develop leadership skills is to learn from others who are already successful leaders. This can be in the form of reading books, attending seminars or conferences, or seeking out a mentor who can provide guidance and support. By studying the leadership styles and techniques of others, you can gain valuable insights and ideas that you can apply to your own leadership development.

3. Reflect on Your Experiences

It is important to reflect on your experiences as a leader in order to learn from them and improve your leadership skills. This can involve asking for feedback from others, analyzing your own behavior and decision-making, and taking the time to reflect on what worked and what didn't in previous leadership experiences. By reflecting on your experiences, you can identify areas for improvement and develop strategies for becoming a more effective leader.

4. Develop Self-Awareness

Developing self-awareness is an important aspect of becoming a true leader. This involves understanding your own strengths and weaknesses, as well as your values, beliefs, and personality traits. By developing self-awareness, you can better understand how you can best lead others and how you can work to improve your leadership skills.

5. Practice Empathy

Empathy is an important characteristic of true leaders, and it is also a skill that can be developed over time. This involves developing the ability to understand and relate to the feelings and experiences of others. By practicing empathy, you can build stronger relationships with your followers and create a more positive and productive work environment.

6. Commit to Lifelong Learning

Becoming a true leader is a lifelong journey that requires a commitment to continuous learning and growth. This involves seeking out new opportunities for learning and development, whether it be through reading, attending seminars or conferences, or seeking out new challenges and experiences. By committing to lifelong learning, you can continue to develop your leadership skills and stay ahead of the curve in an ever-changing world.

Chapter 8 : Conclusion

In conclusion, developing true leadership requires a combination of self-reflection, learning from others, seeking out leadership opportunities, developing self-awareness, practicing empathy, and committing to lifelong learning. By working to develop these skills, individuals can become true leaders who are able to inspire and motivate others towards a common goal, create a positive and productive work environment, and achieve lasting success.

Leadership of convenience can have negative consequences for both the leader and the organization they lead. True, on the other hand, involves a commitment to developing oneself as a leader and creating a positive and productive work environment.

In this book, we have explored the concept of leadership of convenience and its negative consequences. We have also discussed the importance of true leadership and the characteristics that define a true leader. Additionally, we have outlined strategies for developing true leadership skills, including seeking out leadership opportunities, learning from others, reflecting on experiences, developing self-awareness, practicing empathy, and committing to lifelong learning.

It is important to note that developing true leadership skills is a lifelong journey that requires ongoing effort and commitment. However, the benefits of true leadership are numerous, including increased employee satisfaction and productivity, improved organizational performance, and a greater sense of purpose and fulfilment for the leader themselves.

Chapter 9 Self Analysis : Are you a Leader of Convenience?

Instructions: Answer the following questions honestly and assign yourself a score based on the provided scale. Add up your scores at the end to find out if you tend to be a leader of convenience. Remember, this analysis is for self-reflection purposes only.

Score Scale:

1 = Strongly Disagree

2 = Disagree

3 = Neutral

4 = Agree

5 = Strongly Agree

Questions:

1. I often take on leadership roles because it benefits me personally.

2. I am more likely to lead when there are personal advantages involved.

3. I tend to avoid leading when there are challenges or difficulties.

4. I prioritize my own interests over the interests of the group.

5. I am selective about the leadership roles I take on.

6. I feel comfortable delegating tasks to others without getting involved myself.

7. I am less motivated to lead if there is no immediate personal gain.

8. I often look for shortcuts or easier ways to accomplish leadership tasks.

9. I am more likely to lead when there is recognition or praise involved.

10. I avoid taking responsibility for mistakes or failures.

11. I prefer leading when the workload is light or manageable.

12. I tend to withdraw from leadership when there is conflict or disagreement.

13. I am motivated by power and control in leadership positions.

14. I am reluctant to take on leadership if it requires significant effort or sacrifice.

15. I find it easier to lead when others are dependent on me.

16. I prioritize my personal comfort over the growth and development of others.

17. I am more likely to lead when it boosts my social status.

18. I avoid leading when it requires challenging the status quo.

19. I tend to lead only when it aligns with my personal values and beliefs.

20. I lack consistency in my leadership actions and decisions.

21. I feel uneasy when others rely on me for guidance or direction.

22. I prioritize my personal goals over the collective goals of the group.

23. I am more motivated to lead when there are financial benefits involved.

24. I tend to avoid leading when it involves taking risks or facing uncertainty.

25. I am hesitant to lead unless it guarantees personal advantages.

Scoring:

Add up the scores for all the questions you answered and divide it by 5 to obtain your final score out of 25.

Results:

0-10: You are not a leader of convenience. You demonstrate a genuine commitment to leadership and prioritize the collective goals of the group over personal gains.

11-15: You occasionally exhibit characteristics of a leader of convenience. It's important to reflect on your motivations and ensure that your decisions are guided by the best interests of the group.

16-20: You often act as a leader of convenience. It's essential to examine your intentions and work towards developing a more authentic and selfless leadership approach.

21-25: You strongly align with the traits of a leader of convenience. It is crucial to reassess your leadership style and motivations to foster a more genuine and effective leadership approach.

Remember, this is just a self-assessment tool and should be used as a starting point for reflection and improvement. Seeking feedback from others and engaging in ongoing self-reflection and growth can help you to become a more effective and authentic leader.

Thanks!